D1708182

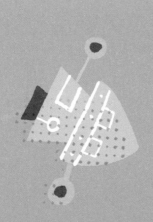

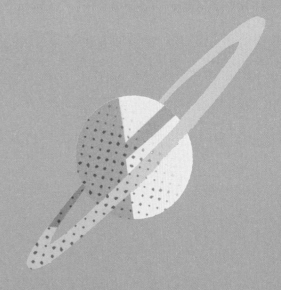

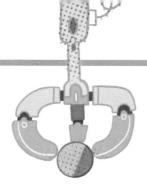

Jobs of the Future

Imaginative Careers for Forward-Thinking Kids

Sofia E. Rossi
& Carlo Canepa

Illustrated by
Luca Poli

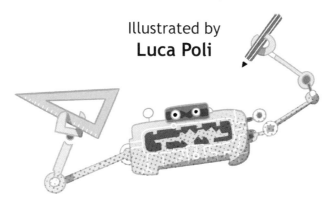

Andrews McMeel
PUBLISHING®

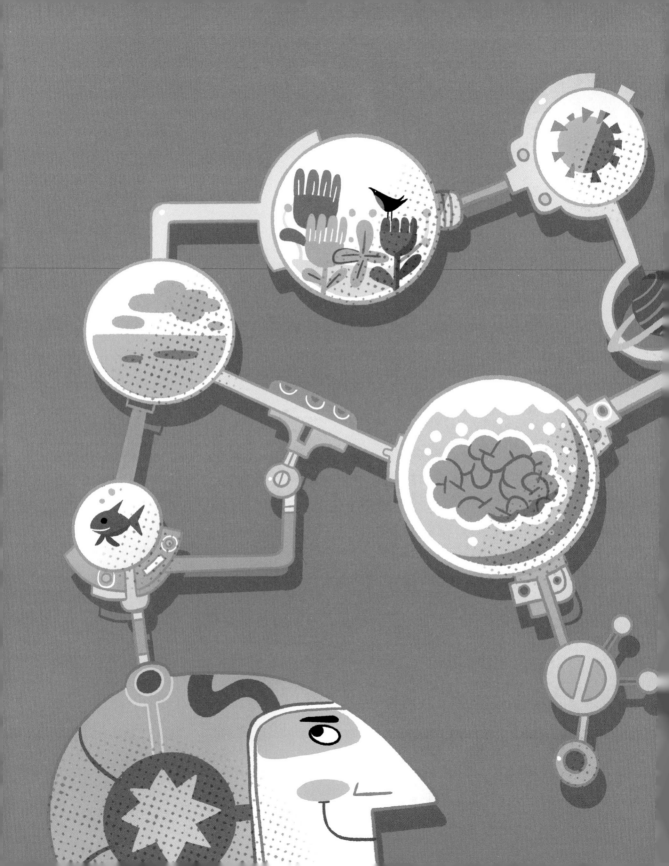

CONTENTS

INTRODUCTION

How many times have you been asked what you want to be when you grow up? And how many times have you not been able to answer because you weren't sure or you weren't interested in doing the same jobs as the adults in your life?

Well, you should know that whatever job you eventually pursue, there's a good chance it doesn't yet exist . . . but it will soon!

In fact, in a few years' time, you may be able to **bring species that have been extinct for millennia back to life**, or you might **build houses** in impossible places. You may even try to **identify diseases** that are unknown today or **communicate with trees**.

Each job of the future has a unique mission and requires a set of **innovative tools** with which to carry it out.

How will the plastics fisherman save the oceans from pollution? Will the **DNA** tailor be able to cut and mend diseased genes? And will the cloud hunter succeed in slowing global warming before it's too late?

You'll find all these answers and more on
this journey of discovery inspired by **physics**
and **biology**, **robotics** and **neuroscience**.
It may be hard to believe, but before too long,
the jobs described in this book will seem as ordinary
as "doctor," "teacher," or "carpenter."

**Very soon, technologies and professions
that sound like they're straight
out of science fiction
will become accessible
to everyone.**

Why not start dreaming
right now?

Let's go!

THE ARCHITECT
OF IMPOSSIBLE
PLACES

"Raising the sidewalks and the streets by 4 inches wasn't good enough. The water is up to my knees again . . . it's even gushing out of the manholes!" Thomas exclaims. As an *architect of impossible places,* he has already found solutions for many cities that were submerged because of the sudden rise in sea levels caused by global warming. His first construction site was on the polar ice. A few years later, he was called to the middle of the Pacific Ocean, where he very quickly managed to build an entire city underwater. Children felt like they were living inside a huge aquarium!

"Unfortunately, we will be forced to build a detachment of the city in a different area of the planet that is still uninhabited," Thomas explains to the mayor.

The chosen location is a region in the central Sahara Desert. With its dried-out streams and sandy dunes, the environment for the new city is extreme, but there is no other alternative.

Wasting no time, the architect of impossible places takes action together with his team of workers. But once they arrive at the city's new location . . . "Someone else is already building here! How is that possible?" Thomas shouts. He has promised the mayor that he would save the city in just a few months, and he cannot afford to delay construction.

Thomas immediately asks for a meeting with the architect already building on the site. She is Italian, from the city of Venice. Faced with the same problem Thomas was, she, too, chose to relocate to the Sahara—one of the least-inhabited places on Earth. After talking it over, the two architects decide to collaborate and combine their knowledge for the benefit of all. And so they quickly come up with a new project that can accommodate the residents of both their cities. No more roads or pollution; transportation will function exclusively through a system of elevated pipes filled with compressed air. There will be plants everywhere, houses will be covered with solar panels, and everything—absolutely everything—will be recycled. •

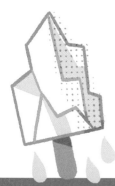

Rise in ocean temperatures: The oceans are 1.2 degrees warmer today than they were in 1950.

- Increased damage related to tides and coastal storms.

- Increased coastal erosion.

- Increased movement of **sediments**, such as sand and pebbles.

WHAT ARE THE LARGEST CONTRIBUTING FACTORS TO RISING SEA LEVELS?

Melting glaciers: Warming ocean temperatures cause over 1,700 trillion pounds of glacial ice to melt into the sea each year.

Land sinkage: Disappearing groundwater and the movement of **tectonic plates** have caused land to sink into the ocean.

THESE ARE THE SHORT-TERM EFFECTS OF RISING SEA LEVELS.

HOW MUCH WILL SEA LEVELS RISE IN THE NEXT FEW YEARS?

According to data collected by scientists in the last few decades, world sea levels have risen 8 to 9 inches since 1880. Some scientists believe that by the year 2100, sea levels may have risen by 3 feet. This means that some cities, such as Venice, Italy, could end up completely underwater.

To prevent further sea level rise, we must slow global warming!

50

30

25

15

0

SKILLS & ATTITUDE CHECKLIST

○ Creativity

○ The ability to think outside the box

○ A passion for physics and mathematics

○ A willingness to cooperate with others

○ An eye for detail

○ Good drawing skills

THE EXPLORER
OF FARAWAY
PLANETS

Outside the porthole, it is -76°F, and a very strong red dust storm is raging. Not exactly the **climate** we are used to on Earth, but, overall, Nellie likes life on Mars.

However, Nellie is an *explorer of faraway planets,* and her mission is to discover and explore new worlds. "The time has come to set off again," she tells her friends. That's because a planet very similar to Earth orbits around the star **Sirius.**

"With our new propeller, it should only take us three days," Nellie declares as she prepares for takeoff with her copilot. "I wonder if this new planet may one day host the human race, just like Mars," she says.

After entering the precise coordinates of the new planet in their spaceship's computer, Nellie and her copilot position themselves on **cryogenic** beds; to avoid

unnecessary physical movement during the flight, the explorers freeze their bodies completely and wake back up just before arrival. "Good night!" Nellie whispers as the darkness of outer space slowly envelops the ship.

Just a little over 10 hours have passed when . . . **OOWEEWEEOO!** The alarm starts sounding, and Nellie wakes up startled. It is extremely hot in the room, and it's getting hotter, according to the temperature-control light.

"Oh, no!" Nellie's copilot screams, pointing at the window behind Nellie. "We're about to crash into that ball of fire!" Nellie whips around to see the star Sirius—a blazing sun—quickly approaching. The temperature outside the spacecraft has already risen to 6,300°F. Nellie knows that the cooling system won't be able to hold up much longer.

"We must've entered the coordinates incorrectly—or we've been knocked off course by a strange gravitational pull!" Nellie exclaims, rushing toward the cockpit.

Just as a crash seems inevitable, Nellie manages to change the ship's course, steering it just far enough away from Sirius to avoid a collision. Sweating, she collapses into her seat. As the temperature in the cockpit begins to lower, she knows they'll make it safely to their destination. •

You are here!

SKILLS & ATTITUDE CHECKLIST

- ◯ Calm in an emergency
- ◯ A passion for astronomy
- ◯ The ability to train hard
- ◯ A love of the stars
- ◯ Curiosity
- ◯ A great desire to travel

WHERE ARE WE WITHIN THE UNIVERSE?

- Earth is part of a solar system that includes eight planets revolving around a sun.

- The solar system is part of the Milky Way, a galaxy that scientists believe could contain up to 400 billion stars.

- The Milky Way is one of more than 100 billion galaxies estimated to exist in the universe!

Sun

Mercury Venus Earth Mars Jupiter Saturn Uranus Neptune

PLANETS AROUND THE UNIVERSE: SOME NUMBERS:

We have already discovered over 3,000 other planet systems in the universe. Currently, more than **4,100** planets are being studied:

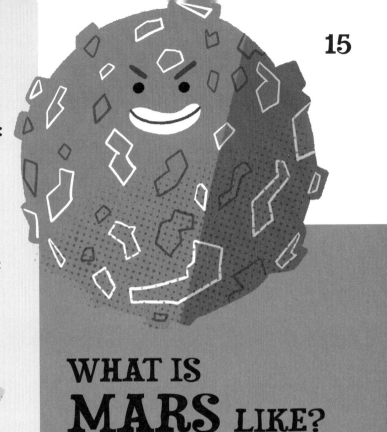

- Almost **1,500** are similar to Neptune.

- More than **1,400** are giant gaseous planets, similar to Jupiter.

- More than **1,300** are "super-Earths," planets that are up to **10 TIMES** the size of Earth.

- Approximately **160** are similar to our planet.

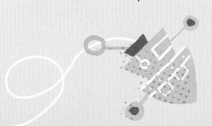

WHAT IS MARS LIKE?

On Mars, the temperature varies between -220°F and 86°F, but the average temperature is around -81.5°F; it's much colder than the North Pole!

Mars is nicknamed the "Red Planet" because the ground and rocks there are full of iron oxide, which gives them their red color. The planet's **atmosphere** is very thin and is composed of 95 percent carbon dioxide.

The way Mars tilts on its axis causes the planet to go through four seasons, just like Earth, but they are much more extreme. For example, winds create huge sandstorms. If caught in one of these storms, astronauts would have a very hard time maintaining any sense of direction!

THE CLOUD HUNTER

It's been years since the clouds have mostly disappeared, leaving the sky almost completely blue. Juan and the other *cloud hunters* miss the time when, as children, they enjoyed imagining what shapes the clouds made: sheep, birds, and many other wonderful animals! Today, Juan and his friends are on a mission to hunt down newly born clouds, trap them, and then scatter them around the world, wherever clouds are scarce. They know that the absence of clouds makes our planet much warmer.

"The clouds keep rising higher in the sky. To reach them, we will be climbing to an **altitude** of almost 20,000 feet! Are you ready?" Juan asks. They have already been to the North Pole, to the Dolomite Mountains in Italy, and to the Swiss Alps, but never to the great mountain ranges of South America. Wearing their helmets and traction cleats, Juan and the cloud hunters are ready for the climb.

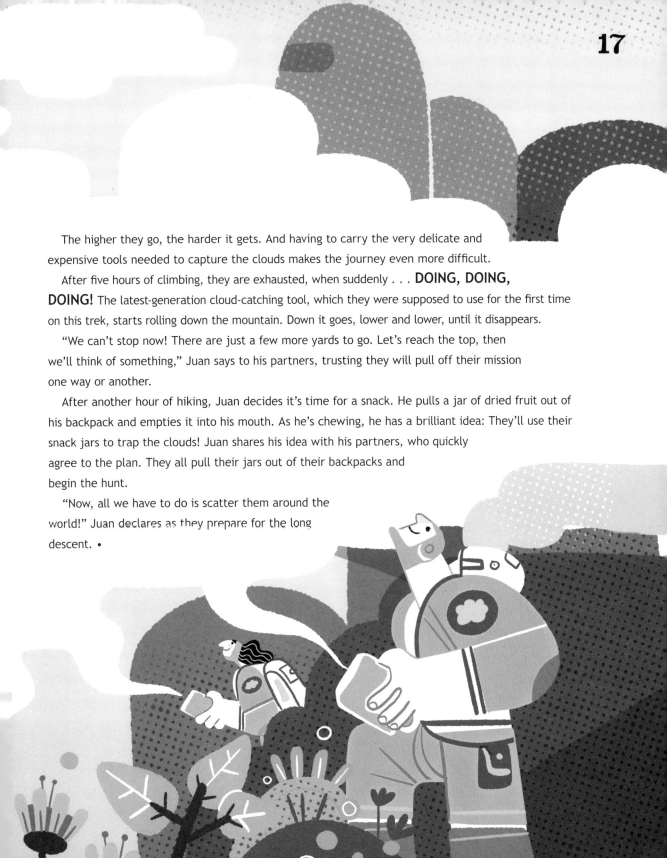

The higher they go, the harder it gets. And having to carry the very delicate and expensive tools needed to capture the clouds makes the journey even more difficult.

After five hours of climbing, they are exhausted, when suddenly . . . **DOING, DOING, DOING!** The latest-generation cloud-catching tool, which they were supposed to use for the first time on this trek, starts rolling down the mountain. Down it goes, lower and lower, until it disappears.

"We can't stop now! There are just a few more yards to go. Let's reach the top, then we'll think of something," Juan says to his partners, trusting they will pull off their mission one way or another.

After another hour of hiking, Juan decides it's time for a snack. He pulls a jar of dried fruit out of his backpack and empties it into his mouth. As he's chewing, he has a brilliant idea: They'll use their snack jars to trap the clouds! Juan shares his idea with his partners, who quickly agree to the plan. They all pull their jars out of their backpacks and begin the hunt.

"Now, all we have to do is scatter them around the world!" Juan declares as they prepare for the long descent. •

HOW MANY TYPES OF CLOUDS ARE THERE IN THE WORLD?

According to the World Meteorological Organization, there are over one hundred types of clouds in the world, all of them different from each other in shape and the altitude above ground in which they are formed. Just as we classify animals and plants, we can group clouds into 10 types.

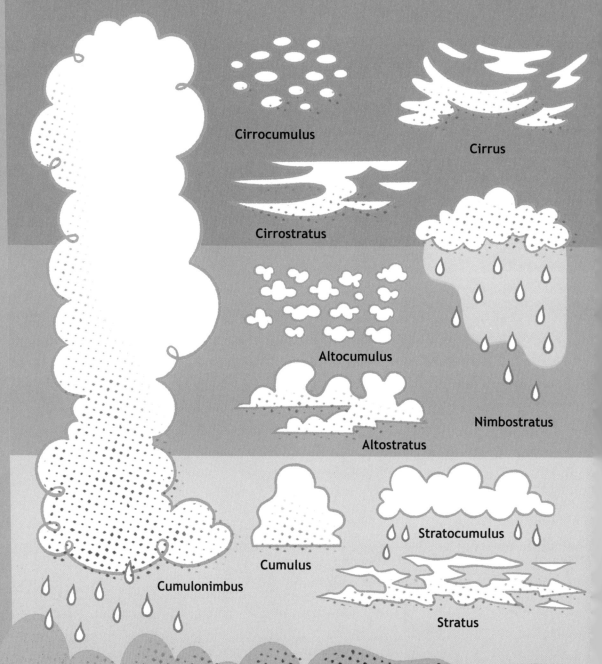

HIGH-ALTITUDE CLOUDS

MEDIUM-ALTITUDE CLOUDS

LOW-ALTITUDE CLOUDS

Cirrocumulus

Cirrus

Cirrostratus

Altocumulus

Nimbostratus

Altostratus

Cumulus

Stratocumulus

Cumulonimbus

Stratus

WHAT ROLE DO CLOUDS PLAY IN THE WARMING OF EARTH?

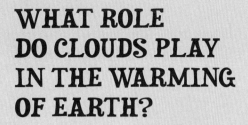

During the day, clouds can make Earth's temperatures cooler by blocking the heat of the sun. At night, they can make Earth's temperatures warmer by trapping the heat of the sun that has accumulated in the ground during the day.

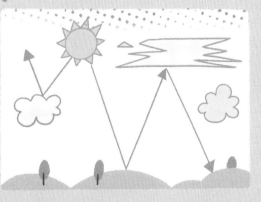

Thin clouds, like cirrus clouds, are found higher up in the atmosphere and generally make an area warmer. Clouds at a lower altitude, like stratus and cumulus, tend to cool areas.

SKILLS & ATTITUDE
CHECKLIST

○ Good climbing skills

○ An interest in climate

○ A love of mountains

○ Head in the clouds

○ A steady hand

○ Indifference to storms

THE PLASTICS FISHERMAN

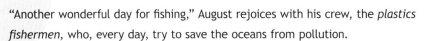

"Another wonderful day for fishing," August rejoices with his crew, the *plastics fishermen,* who, every day, try to save the oceans from pollution.

Thanks to oil, humans have invented a convenient and inexpensive material: plastic. However, once it is abandoned in the environment, plastic is very difficult to get rid of.

August and his crew use a special plastic-catching magnetic net that instantly attracts garbage, leaving the fish free to swim undisturbed.

"Oh no, it's happened again! This is the second time in a week!" shouts August, leaping into the lifeboat. In the distance, he sees the huge wings of an albatross flapping in the water. The creature is squawking loudly; it's clearly in distress.

It takes the crew nearly an hour to untangle the bird from their net, but the effort is well worth it. When the animal is finally free, it soars off into the distance.

In addition to large objects, something invisible and more menacing is hiding in the oceans: dangerous microplastics. Thinner than strands of hair and smaller than grains of sand, when eaten by fish, microplastics end up in our frying pans and on our plates.

And this is where the plastics fishermen's latest invention comes into play.

"Well done, Moby. Let's see how much microplastic you've managed to swallow today," August says, heading toward the ship's stern. There, a blue whale-shaped robot, with hundreds of very long teeth that act as a filter, emerges out of the water. The teeth were built with special materials and are designed to catch only microplastics.

"Not bad! This area is definitely cleaner!" rejoices August. "Now all we need is a good night's sleep. Tomorrow, we're heading south!" •

SKILLS & ATTITUDE
CHECKLIST

○ A passion for the sea

○ A positive attitude

○ An interest in ecology

○ Excellent aim

○ Good swimming skills

○ An awareness of recycling procedures

THAT'S A LOT OF PLASTIC!

In 2018, the U.S. produced

35.7 MILLION
tons of plastic.

Every year, **8 MILLION** metric tons of plastics find their way to our oceans.

THAT'S A LOT OF ANIMALS!

Of the **700** living species that are harmed by plastic in the oceans:

- 35% are birds
- 27% are fish
- 20% are **invertebrates**
- 13% are marine **mammals**
- 5% are **reptiles**

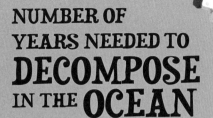

NUMBER OF YEARS NEEDED TO DECOMPOSE IN THE OCEAN

ALBATROSS

"I dived into the water to fish, but I got caught in a plastic net that I didn't see. Fiddlesticks!"

TUNA FISH

"What a silly tuna I am! These microplastics taste like nothing at all!"

TURTLE

"I thought it was a jellyfish, but it was actually a plastic bag!"

Cigarette butt: **10**

Plastic bag: **20**

Can: **200**

Plastic bottle: **450**

Disposable diaper: **450**

Fishing line: **600**

THE PLANT WHISPERER

For some time, the Komi Forest in Russia has been looking sick. Day after day, the leaves are turning yellow, the branches are drying out, and some plant species are even disappearing. Viola and her team of *plant whisperers* arrive to take care of the forest. Actually, "whisperer" may be too simple a word; these researchers have discovered the key to communicating with plants. They are the only ones able to understand what trees, flowers, leaves, and roots say to one another.

"It won't be long before all the trees get permanently sick. Let's get to work!" says Viola. They quickly install the new simultaneous translator Viola created in the laboratory. It receives the plants' languages and translates them into something humans can understand.

The ground detectors begin their work, and soon the first wave sequences begin to appear on the screen. They seem incoherent, but after a few seconds, the words start to make sense. Viola reads the message received from the forest aloud: "Without us and the oxygen that we produce, life on the planet would be impossible. Air pollution and climate change are preventing us from doing our work."

Simple remedies are not enough to cure a vanishing forest, so the whisperers must come up with a drastic solution. "We will create the first and only town in the world built specifically for plants. It will be called Arborea!" Viola exclaims.

"The trees and flowers will receive all the attention they need, thanks to the work of us plant whisperers, and, in return, the plants will produce oxygen for the residents of the nearby cities." •

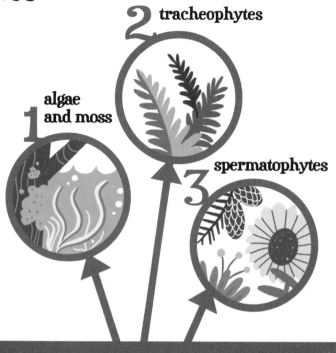

2 tracheophytes

1 algae and moss

3 spermatophytes

HOW ARE PLANTS CLASSIFIED?

SKILLS & ATTITUDE CHECKLIST

○ An excellent knowledge of plants and flowers

○ A love of nature

○ A good sense of direction

○ An appreciation for bees and insects

○ A willingness to get your hands dirty!

○ A talent for solving puzzles and brainteasers

WHAT PUTS THE PLANTS ON OUR PLANET IN DANGER?

FIRES

Fires have always existed in nature, and, at the right frequency, they can help vegetation to regrow and thrive.
But, in recent decades, the number of fires has increased excessively.

GLOBAL WARMING

Human activity is causing:
● An increase in temperatures.
● Increasing rainfall in some areas and dryness in others.
● More carbon dioxide in the atmosphere, rising sea levels, and saltier ocean water.

ILLEGAL TRADE

Just like animals, plants can fall victim to criminals who exploit them for money. Thankfully, over 31,000 plant species are protected by the Convention on International Trade in Endangered Species.

INVASIVE SPECIES

Some plant species, like the common ivy plant, are considered invasive. Removed from their own habitats, they "colonize" environments foreign to them, endangering the plants and animals that live there. Animals, too—especially some types of insects—can become invasive, harming native plant life.

HOW MANY SPECIES OF PLANTS EXIST?

It is estimated that there are about 400,000 plant species in the world—but we haven't yet discovered all of them!

ARE NEW PLANT SPECIES STILL BEING FOUND?

Yes! On average, scientists discover and research approximately 2,000 new plant species every year.

THE **DNA** TAILOR

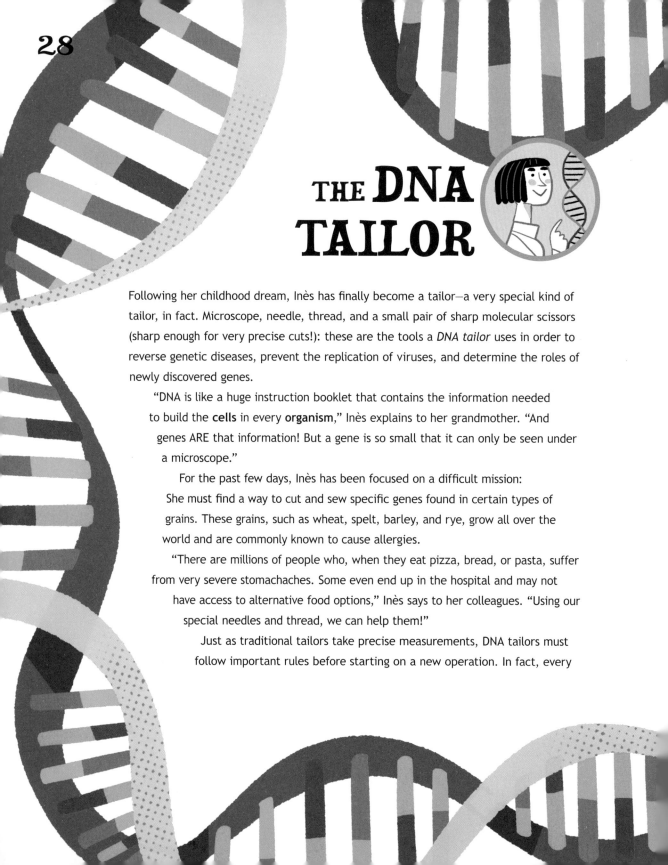

Following her childhood dream, Inès has finally become a tailor—a very special kind of tailor, in fact. Microscope, needle, thread, and a small pair of sharp molecular scissors (sharp enough for very precise cuts!): these are the tools a *DNA tailor* uses in order to reverse genetic diseases, prevent the replication of viruses, and determine the roles of newly discovered genes.

"DNA is like a huge instruction booklet that contains the information needed to build the **cells** in every **organism**," Inès explains to her grandmother. "And genes ARE that information! But a gene is so small that it can only be seen under a microscope."

For the past few days, Inès has been focused on a difficult mission: She must find a way to cut and sew specific genes found in certain types of grains. These grains, such as wheat, spelt, barley, and rye, grow all over the world and are commonly known to cause allergies.

"There are millions of people who, when they eat pizza, bread, or pasta, suffer from very severe stomachaches. Some even end up in the hospital and may not have access to alternative food options," Inès says to her colleagues. "Using our special needles and thread, we can help them!"

Just as traditional tailors take precise measurements, DNA tailors must follow important rules before starting on a new operation. In fact, every

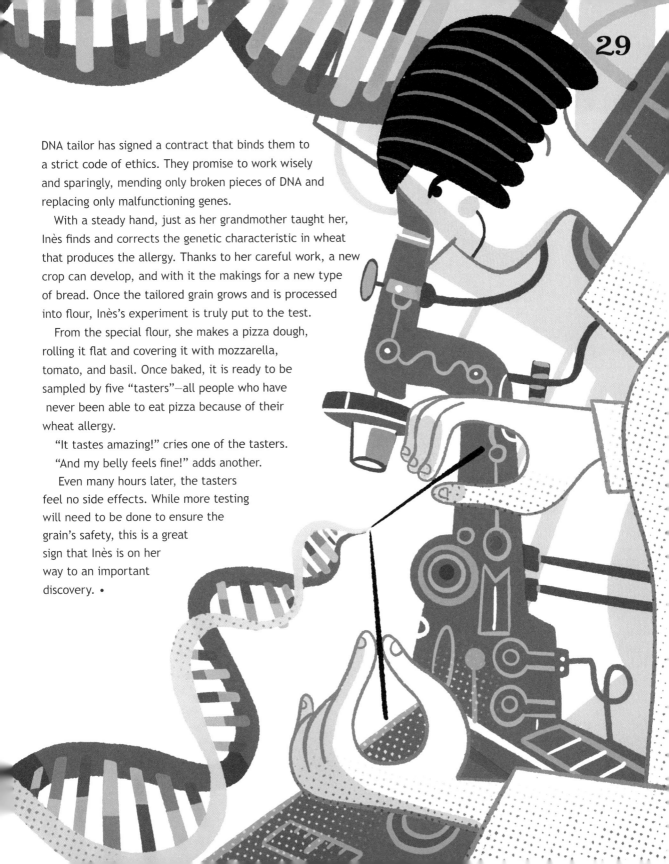

DNA tailor has signed a contract that binds them to a strict code of ethics. They promise to work wisely and sparingly, mending only broken pieces of DNA and replacing only malfunctioning genes.

With a steady hand, just as her grandmother taught her, Inès finds and corrects the genetic characteristic in wheat that produces the allergy. Thanks to her careful work, a new crop can develop, and with it the makings for a new type of bread. Once the tailored grain grows and is processed into flour, Inès's experiment is truly put to the test.

From the special flour, she makes a pizza dough, rolling it flat and covering it with mozzarella, tomato, and basil. Once baked, it is ready to be sampled by five "tasters"—all people who have never been able to eat pizza because of their wheat allergy.

"It tastes amazing!" cries one of the tasters.

"And my belly feels fine!" adds another.

Even many hours later, the tasters feel no side effects. While more testing will need to be done to ensure the grain's safety, this is a great sign that Inès is on her way to an important discovery. •

WHAT IS DNA?

"DNA" stands for "deoxyribonucleic acid." It's like a big book containing instructions for the growth and function of every kind of organism. The alphabet in which this "book" is written is made up of only four letters, arranged along a helix-shaped chain: A, C, T, and G.

Once "unrolled," the DNA contained in each human cell is just over 9 feet long. If you were to link the chains of DNA from all the cells in the human body, you'd have a string that was much, much longer than the distance between Earth and the sun!

SKILLS & ATTITUDE CHECKLIST

○ Extreme precision

○ A passion for biotechnology

○ An interest in very tiny objects

○ A collaborative spirit

○ A knack for sewing, mending, or needlepoint

○ A steady hand

WHAT IS GENETIC EDITING AND HOW DOES IT WORK?

The sequence of letters with which our DNA is written is not always consistent, and irregularities may occur. Scientists are learning to fix these irregularities, thanks to a technique known as genetic editing. Using this technique, they can cut out the DNA that cause certain diseases and replace them with those that don't.

But be careful:

PLAYING AROUND WITH DNA IS NO JOKE!

THE MASTER INVENTOR

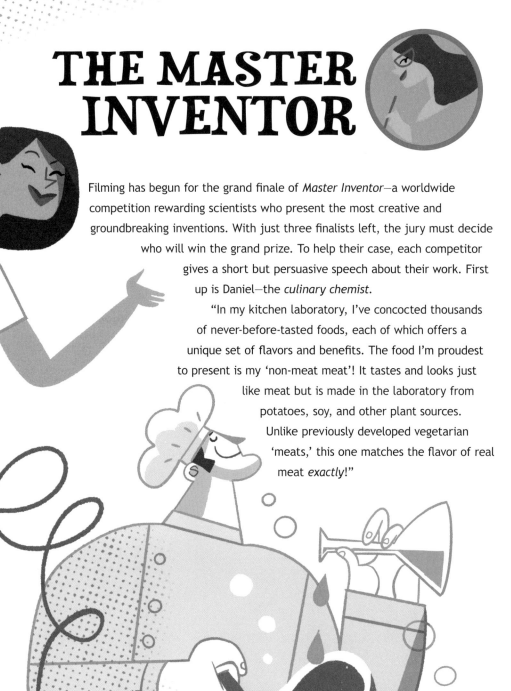

Filming has begun for the grand finale of *Master Inventor*—a worldwide competition rewarding scientists who present the most creative and groundbreaking inventions. With just three finalists left, the jury must decide who will win the grand prize. To help their case, each competitor gives a short but persuasive speech about their work. First up is Daniel—the *culinary chemist*.

"In my kitchen laboratory, I've concocted thousands of never-before-tasted foods, each of which offers a unique set of flavors and benefits. The food I'm proudest to present is my 'non-meat meat'! It tastes and looks just like meat but is made in the laboratory from potatoes, soy, and other plant sources. Unlike previously developed vegetarian 'meats,' this one matches the flavor of real meat *exactly*!"

A chorus of WOWs rises from the audience; the judges look impressed. Will the second contender be able to top Daniel's invention?

Leah—a **textile** biologist—steps forward.

"The animal kingdom is like a living library from which we can draw endless inspiration!" she begins. "After studying chameleons, gray tree frogs, and other color-changing animals for years, I've replicated their camouflaging abilities in a new type of fabric I call chameleo-cloth!" She whips a fabric sample in the air, displaying its impressive ability to change color, matching its environment perfectly.

Now the audience is truly stunned. But there's one competitor who has yet to present: the *molecular sculptor*.

"Have you ever heard of nanotechnology?" Anita asks the crowd. "Every day, I study extremely small molecular fragments—as small as one nanometer in size. That's a hundred thousand times smaller than a single human hair! Using extremely powerful microscopes, I've developed a way to restore ancient structures that were previously destroyed by pollution."

Before-and-after photos of an ancient Egyptian statue appear on the screen behind Anita. In the first photo, the statue is severely damaged and crumbling—and in the second photo, it looks completely new! Using her unique sculpting technique, Anita was able to repair the statue on a molecular level.

The audience gasps in wonder. How will the judges possibly choose a winner? They huddle together to decide.

After a few moments, a drumroll is heard . . . and then: "IT'S A THREE-WAY TIE!" shouts one of the judges. Everyone cheers as the contestants embrace, congratulating one another. For the first time in *Master Inventor* history, the finalists' inventions were so impressive, all three were awarded the grand prize! •

MASTER INVENTORS: TOOLS OF THE TRADE

SKILLS & ATTITUDE CHECKLIST

○ Creative problem-solving ○ Strong observation skills

○ A powerful imagination ○ Aesthetic sensibility

○ Empathy ○ Patience

In the future, science and art will be more closely connected than ever before. Artists such as sculptors, fashion designers, and chefs can look to the latest science to perfect their creations, while chemists and biologists may need the help of artists to think outside the box. And the best inventors will be both scientifically knowledgeable AND artistically inclined!

• WHAT IS SCIENTIFIC CUISINE?

Scientific cuisine combines the art of cooking with a biochemical knowledge of food. Today, we are already working toward scientific cuisine. Research is currently underway to create environmentally friendly "meat" in the laboratory. If scientists can succeed in developing tasty and nutritious meat substitutes, we'll limit our reliance on the harmful beef, pork, and poultry industries.

tools for holding, turning, and cutting

robot sous-chef

high-speed blender

state-of-the-art juicer

extra-sensitive scales

THE CULINARY CHEMIST

liquid nitrogen

pots and pans

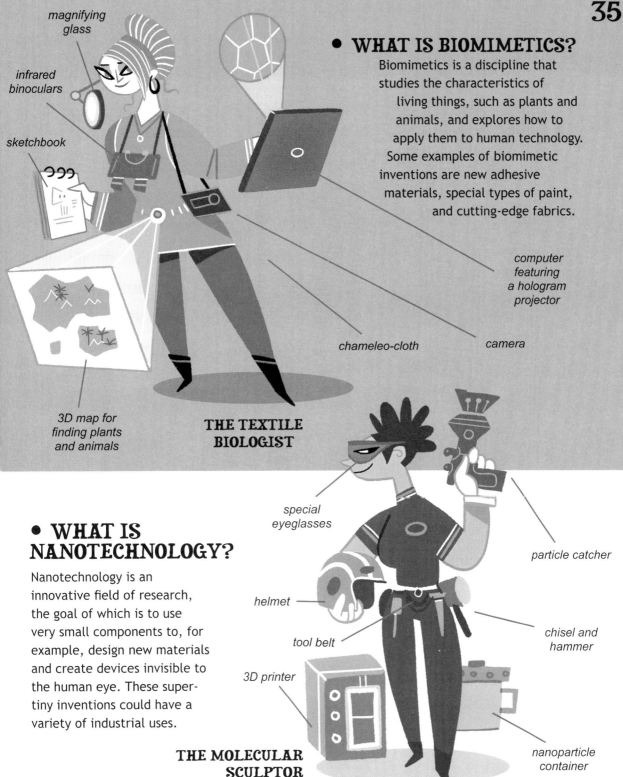

magnifying glass

infrared binoculars

sketchbook

WHAT IS BIOMIMETICS?

Biomimetics is a discipline that studies the characteristics of living things, such as plants and animals, and explores how to apply them to human technology. Some examples of biomimetic inventions are new adhesive materials, special types of paint, and cutting-edge fabrics.

computer featuring a hologram projector

chameleo-cloth

camera

3D map for finding plants and animals

THE TEXTILE BIOLOGIST

special eyeglasses

particle catcher

WHAT IS NANOTECHNOLOGY?

Nanotechnology is an innovative field of research, the goal of which is to use very small components to, for example, design new materials and create devices invisible to the human eye. These super-tiny inventions could have a variety of industrial uses.

helmet

tool belt

chisel and hammer

3D printer

nanoparticle container

THE MOLECULAR SCULPTOR

THE POLAR ICE MAKER

The North Pole isn't what it used to be. Because of rising temperatures, the ice is getting thinner, and more tourists are visiting the Nordic countries' northernmost coastal villages.

Not only does less ice mean fewer fish and birds that love the cold of the North, it also means the area will continue to warm, since the white of the snow and ice helps to reflect away the sun's rays.

However, Emma has been designing a solution for quite awhile now: a sun-powered, ice-shooting submarine that collects water and turns it into small icebergs. Once "released," these icebergs fit together on the ocean's surface, like the pieces of a large puzzle.

This is a bit similar to what ice machines do when they create ice from water. For this reason, Emma has been nicknamed the *polar ice maker*.

Slowly, the icebergs weld together, giving rise to long, white expanses as far as the eye can see. But, lately, something mysterious has been happening: many of the icebergs created by the submarine have been disappearing! One night, Emma decides to hide out in her submarine, parking it just beneath the water's surface near the shore. She's determined to find out what goes on while everyone is asleep.

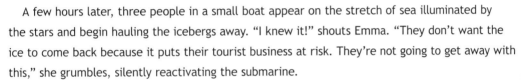

A few hours later, three people in a small boat appear on the stretch of sea illuminated by the stars and begin hauling the icebergs away. "I knew it!" shouts Emma. "They don't want the ice to come back because it puts their tourist business at risk. They're not going to get away with this," she grumbles, silently reactivating the submarine.

Emma steers to the area where the thieves are and positions herself directly beneath them. Using her submarine, she releases several small icebergs at once, programming them to form a "cage" at the surface. Before they know it, the crooks are trapped by the very ice they were attempting to steal! Meanwhile, Emma calls the authorities.

When the village locals learn what Emma has done, they thank her for her important service. Even leaders from around the globe congratulate her, praising her efforts to restore the ice, which is vital to life all over the world. •

THE PLANET'S
AIR CONDITIONER

Polar ice caps are important for climate regulation around the world. The Arctic works as Earth's air conditioner; its ice helps keep the planet cold by reflecting the light and heat of the sun back into space. Less ice means a warmer climate and more extreme weather events.

SKILLS & ATTITUDE
CHECKLIST

- ( ) An interest in climate change
- ( ) A love of arctic and antarctic creatures like polar bears and penguins
- ( ) A love of snow
- ( ) The ability to withstand extreme cold
- ( ) A passion for puzzles
- ( ) An interest in diving

HOW MUCH ICE?

1.2 TRILLION

tons of ice melt in the world every year, including:

- **286** billion tons from Greenland and the Arctic.

- **127** billion tons from Antarctica.

- **335** billion tons from glaciers.

1979

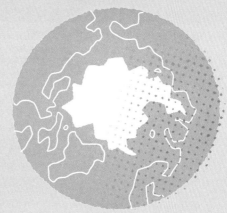

2018

HOW QUICKLY IS THE ARCTIC SHRINKING?

THE PROGRAMMER OF CONSCIOUS ROBOTS

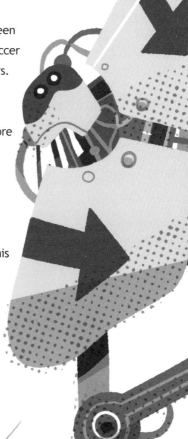

For days, everyone at the university has been talking about Luis's work. He is finally ready to test months and months of hard research toward his goal: the creation of a robot capable of solving problems and moving freely—without human guidance. Luis, along with his fellow *programmers of conscious robots*, has discovered that the only way to reveal the secrets of the human brain and "share" them with robots is to study our brain waves during sleep.

Thanks to a dream-catching pillow he developed, Luis has been analyzing the thoughts, dreams, and memories of dozens of soccer players for months and recording them on a series of computers. Once ready, the information collected will be transferred to Chris7, a special soccer-playing robot.

"Check this out," Luis says to his colleague just minutes before the decisive experiment. "During some stages of sleep, our minds work harder than when we're awake. New ideas come to us, unnecessary thoughts are eliminated, and important memories are strengthened." His colleague nods, patting Luis on the back. "It's gonna go great!" he says.

Everything is ready: Luis begins downloading the data from his special pillow. On the university soccer field are a goalkeeper and three defenders who are waiting to see Chris7 in action. Trembling with excitement, Luis enters the code to activate

the robot: 1-5-4-6. ACCESS DENIED. He tries again: 1-5-4-7. ACCESS DENIED. 1-4-5-8. ACCESS DENIED. Luis breaks into a cold sweat. With all the fuss, he's forgotten the correct sequence of numbers. But just as he is about to throw in the towel and apologize, something incredible happens. Chris7 starts to move forward with the ball. No one has taught him what movements to make—he is acting freely based on the many dreams that Luis has uploaded to his memory. The first defender tries to stop him with a slide, but Chris7 jumps over him with a two-step. He then nutmegs the ball between the second opponent's legs. The third defender tries to intervene, but Chris7 dribbles past him with ease. He finds himself alone in front of the goalkeeper. In the stands, Luis is jumping out of his skin. *Will he be able to score?* Luis thinks to himself. No sooner than Luis asks the question, Chris7 gives the ball a powerful kick, launching it into the corner of the goal!

"We did it!" exclaims Luis, embracing his colleague. "But this is only the first, small step," he adds. "Human consciousness is still a very mysterious **phenomenon**."

"Indeed," says the colleague. "Who knows how many hundreds of surprises our research still has in store for us!" •

STUDYING THE HUMAN BRAIN

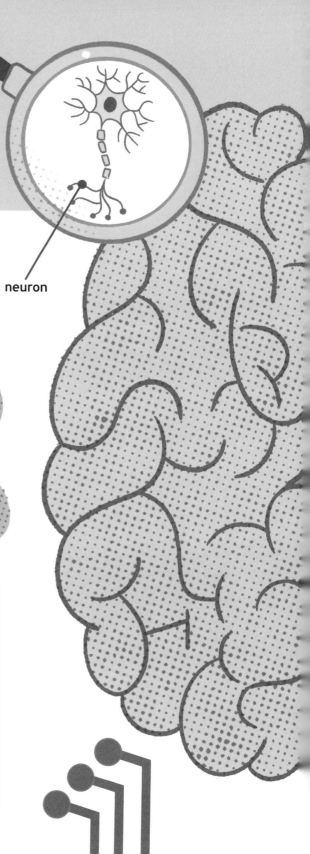

neuron

The brain is one of the most mysterious organs in the human body. Studies of the brain have revealed the structures and processes behind memory, language, sleep, and many other secrets that may one day be used to create increasingly intelligent robots. But there's a long road ahead of us, so let's roll up our sleeves!

The human brain is composed of billions and billions of neurons: tiny nerve cells that process and transmit information at a speed of almost 330 feet per second!

SKILLS & ATTITUDE CHECKLIST

- ○ A passion for computer science
- ○ The ability to learn from your own mistakes
- ○ Willpower
- ○ An interest in neurology
- ○ A love of mathematics
- ○ Experience playing video games

electric
circuit

WHAT ROBOTS
ARE WE USING TODAY?

Today, we have tons of smart computers and robots of all kinds, ranging from the very large to the miniscule. The areas where robots are used vary, but they include:

● **Medicine,** to aid doctors in hospitals during surgery.

● **Industry,** to perform tiring and repetitive tasks.

● **Social relations,** to assist people with disabilities in their everyday lives.

SOME NUMBERS

Growth of the robotics industry in recent years:

2005: Less than 1 million robots.

2016: 1.8 million robots.

2019: 2.6 million robots.

2022: An estimated 3.9 million robots.

THE WATERLESS FARMER

"That's five tomatoes and one basket of strawberries," says Laila as she bags her customer's items.

Fruits and vegetables are a novelty on Mars, so the line for Laila's farm stand is always long.

Back on Earth, Laila was a traditional farmer. She loved growing her own produce and selling it at the local farmer's market. When she arrived on Mars, she knew she would have to develop a new **cultivation** technique.

"On Mars, there's almost no oxygen or water, and the ground is rocky and full of toxic substances," Laila explains to the next customer in line. "That's why I've created something totally new!"

Her method involves growing fruits and vegetables without having to water them or plant them in the ground. Instead, she uses a spray bottle to put essential nutrients directly onto the roots of the produce. For this reason, she's called *the waterless farmer*. So far, her operation has been a huge success, but Laila isn't quite satisfied. In the pocket of her jumpsuit, she keeps some watermelon seeds her grandfather left her. The watermelon was her favorite fruit to grow and sell on Earth, and she dreams of bringing its juicy sweetness to the people of Mars.

One night, after her customers have gone, Laila sets to work cultivating her grandfather's watermelon seeds. But, after several weeks of careful tending, the melons fail to flourish. Instead of the large, colorful fruits Laila remembers, the seeds produce small blue ones no bigger than apples. Laila did not consider an important characteristic of watermelons: they're composed almost entirely of . . . water! And water on Mars, as everyone knows, is incredibly scarce.

Disheartened, Laila crouches down beside her pitiful harvest.

"What's the matter, Laila?" a friend calls, approaching. "What's that strange, blue fruit?"

Before Laila can stop her, her friend plucks one of the melons, cracks it open, and takes a bite. Laila is mortified. This is surely the end of her farming career.

"Oh, my!" says her friend. "This is amazing! How many can I buy?"

Shocked, Laila jumps up. "Have them all!" she says. "And share them! I wanted to grow a watermelon, but I guess I created the first . . . Martian melon!" Laughing, Laila's friend gathers all she can carry, promising to share the bounty with her neighbors. •

WHAT DOES "DROUGHT" MEAN?

A drought is a period of dryness that occurs when there is a prolonged shortage of water, most often due to lack of rainfall. During a drought, the soil is deprived of the liquid and nutrients needed for the growth of plants.

WHAT **EFFECTS** CAN **DROUGHT** HAVE?

Because of global warming and **deforestation**, periods of drought have become longer and more intense in many parts of the planet. Areas that rarely saw drought in the past are now beginning to feel its effects.

SKILLS & ATTITUDE CHECKLIST

- ◯ A green thumb
- ◯ A fondness for fruits and vegetables
- ◯ An enterprising spirit
- ◯ A passion for water conservation
- ◯ An interest in agriculture
- ◯ Excellent problem-solving skills

WHAT CAN WE DO IN ORDER TO AVOID WASTING WATER?

Water is an essential resource that is already at risk of disappearing in many areas of the world. However, there are several simple precautions we can all take in order to limit water waste. Here are just a few:

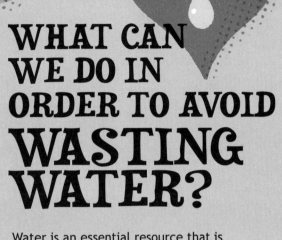

- Limit water use in the home by taking shorter showers (or taking baths instead!), watering our lawns less often, or turning the faucet off while we wash dishes or brush our teeth.

- Invest in environmentally friendly technologies such as high-efficiency washing machines, water-saving shower heads, or composting toilets.

- Reuse and recycle water wherever we can! Harvest rainwater to use for watering plants, or collect clean bathwater to use later for soaking dirty dishes.

THE VIRUS DETECTIVE

Every year in early spring, the streets of Manaus—a Brazilian city on the banks of the Amazon River—are lined with food stalls and filled with dancers swaying to the rhythm of the **samba.**

"The Brazilian **Carnival** is truly a sight to behold," Maya observes, admiring the dancers' ornate costumes.

Maya is a world-famous *virus detective,* known for her incredible ability to locate and identify the microscopic organisms that can cause outbreaks of disease in humans. She's been called to Manaus for just this purpose.

"You see, detective," the mayor of Manaus had explained over the phone, "during the first few days of celebrations, many people began to experience bizarre headaches accompanied by a strange rash, and some of those people have had to be hospitalized. We're concerned that if this unknown virus continues to spread, we'll have more cases than we can treat!"

Maya is certain that the people of Manaus are infected with a new disease. Never before in her career has she encountered a virus that caused these specific symptoms or that spread so rapidly.

When on missions, Maya always carries her VRS ray gun—a tool she developed that helps her identify new viruses in the blood of sick people. Thankfully, several ill Carnival-goers volunteer to be tested. Once she has enough samples, Maya can upload the data to her smartphone, where a special app reproduces the virus in 3D. Right away, Maya can see from the structure of the virus that it must have originated with bats.

"An infected bat must have come in contact with a piece of fruit, which was then sold in the stalls," Maya explains.

Several of the city's physicians are listening and taking notes.

"We'll need to visit the bat caves at the city's edge and perform more tests in order to learn how this virus works," Maya goes on. "Then we can get to work developing a treatment!"

Maya's work will be crucial to stopping the spread of this virus, but it's only one piece of the puzzle. **Deforestation** in the area is a major cause of new viruses. As cities like Manaus expand, animals in the surrounding rain forest lose their natural habitat. For this reason, humans are more often in contact with wild animals, making disease much more common. •

WHAT IS A VIRUS?

Viruses are extremely small and invisible to the naked eye. That is why they can only be observed with an **electron microscope**!

- The **nucleus** of a cell contains genetic material.

- The external protective layer of a cell is called a plasma membrane.

- Special proteins allow the virus to enter cells and infect them.

TYPES OF VIRUSES

Not all viruses are the same! They can have many different shapes, depending on the type of cells they infect (white blood cells, liver cells, nerve cells, etc.) and also the type of disease they cause.

HOW TO STUDY A VIRUS SAFELY

Eye protection

An air-filtering mask for the nose and mouth

Waterproof suit

Long gloves

Shoe covers

SOME RECOMMENDATIONS FOR CONTAINING INFECTION

● Wash your hands often with soap and water.

● Do not touch your eyes, nose, or mouth.

● Cover your mouth if you cough or sneeze.

Avoid crowded locations.

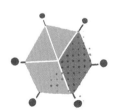
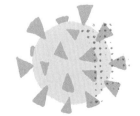

SKILLS & ATTITUDE CHECKLIST

○ An investigative spirit

○ An interest in human biology

○ Compassion

○ A willingness to travel often

○ No fear of needles

○ Extreme precision

THE SUN SAILOR

Seawater crashes against the sides of Peter's boat, sending up a gentle spray.

"It's a good thing I grew up sailing!" Peter says to his first mate. "It's the one form of transportation that hasn't changed!"

In recent years, a transportation revolution has taken place on land and in the air. Now, cars, motorcycles, trains, and airplanes are all powered by renewable energy sources, from **biofuels** and hydropower to solar and wind energy. In fact, when he isn't out at sea, Peter has been working with a team of scientists to develop a new type of land vehicle: the sail-car! It's like a regular car but powered by solar sails that capture and retain the sun's energy, using it to set the car in motion.

Just as the wind picks up, Peter receives a text message from one of his scientist colleagues: *We need your help, Peter!* it reads. *Our solar sail is damaged, and we have an important demonstration this afternoon. Can you be here soon?*

"All right, everyone!" Peter calls to his crew. "We're needed back on land. Full sail ahead for the port!"

Once ashore, Peter heads straight for the lab. Solar sails must be handled with extreme care. That's why experienced *sun sailors* like Peter are called to perform repairs.

"Remember that sails can easily tear or become entangled," Peter explains to his colleagues in the lab. "The thinner the sail, the more carefully it must be furled and unfurled. And these solar sails are extremely thin!"

The scientists watch in awe as Peter swiftly and expertly mends the sail by hand.

"There," he says. "That should do it!"

"Thank you, Peter," says one of his colleagues, pulling him aside. "Would you like to stay and see the sail-car demonstration?"

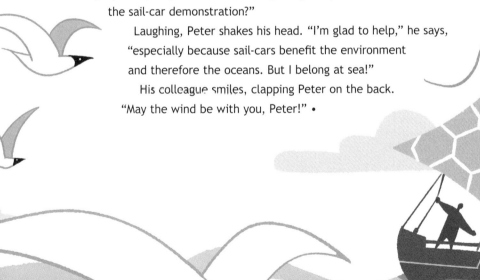

Laughing, Peter shakes his head. "I'm glad to help," he says, "especially because sail-cars benefit the environment and therefore the oceans. But I belong at sea!"

His colleague smiles, clapping Peter on the back.

"May the wind be with you, Peter!" •

WHAT IS RENEWABLE ENERGY?

Renewable energy, as the name suggests, comes from sources that cannot run out, unlike oil and coal. The main types of renewable energy used to produce electricity and heat are:

• SOLAR ENERGY,
which uses the sun's rays.

• WIND ENERGY,
which uses the power of the wind.

• HYDROELECTRIC ENERGY,
which uses the power of water.

• GEOTHERMAL ENERGY,
which comes from the heat produced by Earth.

SKILLS & ATTITUDE CHECKLIST

○ Interest in engineering and chemistry

○ A passion for the environment

○ A love of sailing

○ Precise mending skills

○ A taste for adventure

○ Teamwork

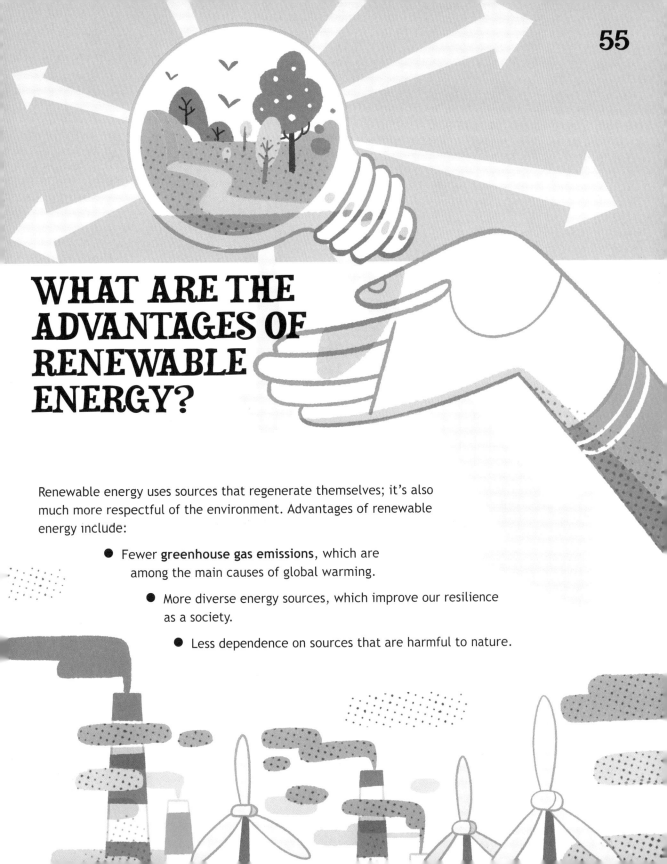

WHAT ARE THE ADVANTAGES OF RENEWABLE ENERGY?

Renewable energy uses sources that regenerate themselves; it's also much more respectful of the environment. Advantages of renewable energy include:

- Fewer **greenhouse gas emissions**, which are among the main causes of global warming.
- More diverse energy sources, which improve our resilience as a society.
- Less dependence on sources that are harmful to nature.

THE CLONER OF THE PAST

"All out of honey and lemons," Francis sighs, crossing those items off his shopping list. Looking around the store, Francis notices that honey and lemons aren't the only missing products. The produce section looks nearly empty!

Over the past few months, bees and other **pollinators** have been disappearing, and with them many of the plant-based foods we eat every day. Even animal feed has become scarce, which means less milk and less meat for everyone.

Francis, who works as a *cloner of the past*, takes this very seriously. He begins making calls, and within a couple of hours, the Sixth Extinction Crisis Unit has assembled in the laboratory.

With the calm coolness that distinguishes him, Francis prepares all the tools necessary to extract DNA from preserved honeybee cells. The goal is to reproduce the DNA **artificially** and bring the missing insects back to life.

After several hours, the cloning technology is beginning to work. "Hey, look!" Francis shouts. "The eggs in the hive are beginning to hatch!"

But something isn't quite right. Some bees have ten legs instead of the usual six. "Maybe this is an advantage," says one of the other cloners of the past. "Ten-legged bees might be able to carry more pollen from one flower to another."

"That's an interesting point," says Francis, "but it's important that the species we release into nature is identical to the original. Even the slightest modification could have a huge impact."

Following a short discussion, all agree with Francis. Bringing extinct species back to life is a risky job that should be undertaken only when absolutely necessary. And even then, scientists must be very careful not to upset nature's harmony.

"We'll have to keep trying," concludes Francis. "And in the meantime, we must focus on protecting what we have. Every creature on Earth plays an important role in our **ecosystem**. Cloners of the past can help, but we aren't the solution!" •

HOW MANY SPECIES ARE AT RISK?

According to the International Union for the Conservation of Nature, more than 38,500 plant and animal species are at risk of extinction today. That's 28 percent of all assessed species!

Among the species analyzed, those most at risk of disappearing forever within the next 20 years are:

THE KOALA
THE SUMATRAN RHINO
THE ESPAÑOLA GIANT-TORTOISE
THE HARLEQUIN FROG

WHAT HAPPENED IN THE PAST?

Some scientists call the period we are living in now the sixth extinction crisis, because there have already been five very large extinction events in the past. The first occurred 440 million years ago, when nearly nine out of every 10 living species were lost. The most recent great extinction occurred 66 million years ago, most likely due to a massive **meteorite** that crashed into Earth and devastated the environment.

SKILLS & ATTITUDE CHECKLIST

- A cool head
- A passion for dinosaurs and other extinct species
- An interest in fossils
- Precision
- A desire to help others
- Patience

ALL IS NOT LOST!

True, the situation is serious, but we must not lose hope. In recent decades, hundreds of projects have begun around the world to protect the most endangered species on Earth. In fact, a study published in 2020 shows that up to 48 species have been saved from extinction since 1993.

THE AIR SWEEPER

As the siren sounds, Amir puts on his suit and gloves, fastens his helmet, and mounts his hoverboard. Together with his team of *air sweepers,* Amir's job is to suck **pollutants** from the air using a solar-powered vacuum cleaner and then pump them through a long carbon pipe that leads to Earth's molten core.

After hovering among the skyscrapers of Delhi, India, all morning, Amir returns to land, flying alongside birds as he cruises through the last banks of clouds.

SCRREEEECH! "Oh, no!" cries Amir. "A bird must've gotten stuck in the vacuum!" He checks the suction nozzle, but there's nothing there. "Locate suctioned object!" Amir shouts, hoping the voice assistant in his helmet will know what to do.

"The suctioned pollutants are nearing headquarters, where they will be filtered in order to stimulate plant growth in the Great Greenhouse," the voice assistant explains. "Any waste or foreign objects will then be sent to the center of the earth, where they will remain forever."

The interactive map inside Amir's visor immediately indicates the position of the bird, just a few feet from the entrance to the Great Greenhouse. "Oh no, it can't end up underground!" shouts Amir as he flies at full speed toward headquarters.

Soon, Amir finds himself at the entrance to an enormous glass house. As he opens the door, he becomes immersed in a thick, green jungle. Stunned by the number and variety of plants he sees, Amir struggles to stay focused on his mission.

Suddenly, he spots a trail of feathers on the greenhouse floor. Following the trail, he eventually spies a beautiful swallow perched on a branch. Its plumage is quite ruffled, and the swallow looks a bit dazed, but it's chirping happily.

Relieved, Amir flies toward the greenhouse ceiling. Opening a small hatch in the roof, he beckons for the swallow, which soars through the opening. "Looks like I'm not the only one who got myself into trouble today," jokes Amir, watching as the bird disappears into the sky. •

CAREFUL WITH THESE SUBSTANCES!

When found in the air at higher concentrations than normally occur in nature, pollutants have a harmful effect on the environment.

These are some of the most common air pollutants:

- **Particulates:** Extremely small liquid droplets that may contain chemicals, soil or dust particles, or allergens such as pollen and mold.

- **Heavy Metals:** Naturally occurring metals such as mercury and lead that are much heavier than water and are highly toxic.

- **Ozone:** A gas that normally exists in the **stratosphere** but is sometimes produced closer to the earth's surface, where it can have harmful health effects.

- **Nitrogen dioxide:** A poisonous gas that most often results from the production of fertilizers.

- **Benzene:** A chemical component of gasoline.

WHERE DOES POLLUTION COME FROM?

Air pollution is mainly caused by humans but also by natural phenomena.

Human sources:
- Air and road traffic
- Household heating
- Agriculture
- Industry
- Construction
- Energy and waste production

Natural sources:
- Volcanoes
- Fires
- Sandstorms

In recent decades, many positive changes have occurred. For example, in Europe, the concentration of some of these substances in the air has been greatly reduced, even halved! However, it's important to keep working to reduce air pollution. Many parts of the world still suffer from dangerously high levels.

WHAT CAN WE DO?

Reducing atmospheric pollution is a concrete and achievable goal. We will need to change our lifestyle habits a little, but the benefits will far outweigh any inconvenience. The four most effective ways to reduce air pollution are:

● Investing in renewable energy, such as solar and wind power.

● Traveling less by car, choosing instead to walk, use a bicycle, or take public transportation such as buses and subways.

● Reducing agricultural and industrial waste.

● Preventing and containing fires.

SKILLS & ATTITUDE CHECKLIST

○ A desire to fly

○ A love of fresh air

○ Cleanliness

○ No fear of heights

○ A desire to help those suffering from pollution-related illness

THE DEEP BLUE DIVER

For months, Ari has been preparing to photograph a very obscure animal: the dragonfish, which lives in the deepest depths of the Pacific Ocean. Despite its name, the dragonfish is very small. It's also rarely ever seen. According to Ari's calculations, this fascinating creature emerges from **trenches** in the ocean floor only once every 100 years.

"Roger, can you hear me? I'm entering the ocean's dark zone," Ari says to his coworker over the radio.

Ari, the deep blue diver, is aboard his trusty submarine Nemo, a dome-shaped, transparent vessel built to withstand extreme pressure. Ari uses its 10 remote-controlled robotic "arms" to walk along the seabed and navigate obstacles. Sitting in the cockpit, Ari has a breathtaking view of the deepest sea. At a depth of 3,300 feet, all radio contact is lost, but Ari likes it that way. Without any distractions, he can focus entirely on the creatures of the **abyss**. *After years of research, we know so much about the moon and the planets, but we've barely explored the oceans . . . and there's so much we have yet to learn!* Ari thinks to himself.

But there is still no trace of the dragonfish. All Ari knows about the fish is that it lives anywhere between 1,600 and 6,000 feet beneath the ocean's surface, and it tends to appear near heat sources. "There has to be a hot gas leak somewhere down here. Nemo, record the temperature in this area," Ari orders the submarine. The temperature gauge attempts a reading, but it struggles to land at a number. The gauge itself quivers, and a sudden rumble knocks Ari out of his seat. Coming to, he realizes that a massive underwater volcano is erupting not 20 feet behind him!

Red-hot lava begins to spew from the volcano's mouth and creep across the seabed. Ari knows he's in danger, but he has no intention of leaving—this could be his only chance to photograph one of the least-seen fish in the sea!

Finally, he spots it: the dragonfish! The long, eel-like creature glows blue amid streams of lava and giant gas bubbles. Its large jaw is lined with impressive fangs. Ari turns off all of Nemo's lights and extends one of its robotic arms to photograph the mysterious fish up close.

CLICK! CLICK! CLICK! "I got the shot!" Ari rejoices. But a smoldering flow of lava is now just inches from the submarine. "Full speed ahead, Nemo!" shouts Ari, commanding the ship to begin its ascent. In seconds, he is several feet above the lava, hurtling toward safety at the ocean's surface. •

UNDER THE DEEP BLUE

The marine environment can be divided into different zones, based on depth.

655 feet

3,300 feet

13,100 feet

23,000 feet

SUNLIGHT ZONE:

Here, we find ourselves near the surface of the ocean, where there is enough light to allow **photosynthesis**.

plankton

clownfish

TWILIGHT ZONE:

Light diminishes more and more.

great white
shark

MIDNIGHT ZONE:

The sun's rays can't reach these ocean depths, and many creatures create light for themselves through a mechanism known as **bioluminescence**.

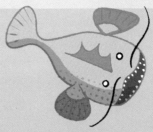

monkfish

ABYSSAL ZONE:

Here, the temperature is close to freezing, and very few animals can survive the extreme water pressure.

sea pig

ULTRA-ABYSSAL ZONE:

We have reached the most mysterious region of the ocean. Despite its extreme conditions, this part of the ocean hosts a surprising number of organisms. Because they are located at such great depths, little is known about these creatures.

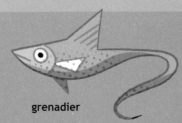

grenadier

Because the world's oceans are so vast and so deep, we aren't sure how many species inhabit our seas! Scientists estimate that over 90 percent of living marine species have yet to be discovered, and 95 percent of the oceans' waters are still unexplored.

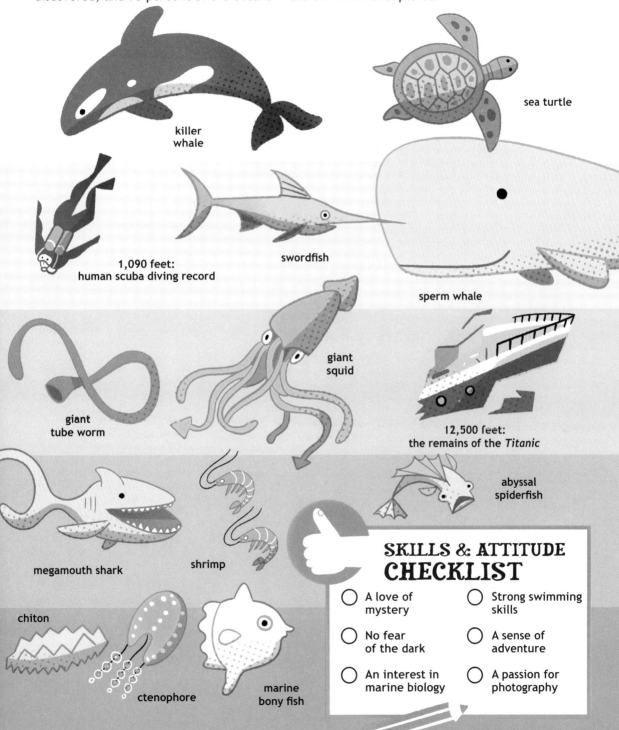

killer whale

sea turtle

1,090 feet: human scuba diving record

swordfish

sperm whale

giant squid

giant tube worm

12,500 feet: the remains of the *Titanic*

megamouth shark

shrimp

abyssal spiderfish

chiton

ctenophore

marine bony fish

SKILLS & ATTITUDE CHECKLIST

- ○ A love of mystery
- ○ No fear of the dark
- ○ An interest in marine biology
- ○ Strong swimming skills
- ○ A sense of adventure
- ○ A passion for photography

THE ALIEN SPOTTER

For hours, the sun has been beating down on the Australian Outback—a desert that covers most of the continent.

Keira the *alien spotter* is lurking behind a large boulder. Now on hour three of her stakeout, she's wearing her protective sun hat and holding a powerful pair of binoculars. But Keira isn't hiding from "aliens." She's hiding from people who may want to harm them!

When Keira talks to others about her job, they often think she wanders through space in search of actual aliens—little green monsters with antennae, four eyes, and flying saucers. But Keira's work takes place entirely on Earth. The "aliens" she spots are not monsters but plant and animal species that have been removed from their natural habitats. Some were transported by humans, while others may have migrated because of climate change.

"It may seem like a small thing," Keira whispers into her handheld recorder, "but the introduction of alien species can cause big problems for nature."

Keira is famous in Australia for developing a new way of dealing with a particular alien species: the dromedary. Dromedaries—large, one-humped camels—may have originated in present-day Somalia or on the Arabian **Peninsula**, and today, they are native throughout the **arid** regions of Africa and central and southwestern Asia. However, in the mid-nineteenth century, explorers shipped large groups of these camels to Australia. Today, dromedaries number in the hundreds of thousands on the island, but, because of rising temperatures and continuous fires, they are running out of water. Agitated and thirsty, they move in droves across the country, causing damage to villages and homes.

Some would prefer to eliminate these animals through a process of **culling**, but for years now, Keira has been working on a new technique. Using a special inflatable pool filled with water, she attracts the dromedaries to the middle of the desert. Once she's captured them, she transports them to a large, protected park, where they can live peacefully with plenty of food and water.

"Here they come!" Keira whispers into her recorder, jumping out from behind the boulder. "I haven't seen 10 such parched dromedaries in a long time," she notes sadly. "Let's allow them to drink awhile before getting them to safety." •

ALIENS IN SIGHT!

Even if they are known as "aliens," invasive species are not trying to start a war. They only want to build themselves a home. Unfortunately, however good their intentions, they represent a threat to native species by altering the balance in their adopted ecosystem!

▲ **WATER HYACINTH**
plant
Origin: the Amazon
New habitat: all over the world!
Characteristics: Water hyacinths grow in thick layers on top of water, blocking light and preventing photosynthesis by other aquatic plants.

▲ **ASIAN GIANT HORNET**
invertebrate
Origin: Asia
New habitat: Europe and North America
Characteristics: The Asian giant hornet eats honeybees, which are needed for the pollination of plants.

▲ **LIONFISH**
fish
Origin: Indian and South Pacific oceans
New habitat: Atlantic Ocean, Gulf of Mexico, and Mediterranean and Caribbean seas
Characteristics: The lionfish has very few predators outside of its home habitat and is a very aggressive predator itself. Its presence in the Atlantic, Gulf of Mexico, and Caribbean puts precious coral reefs at risk.

SKILLS & ATTITUDE CHECKLIST

- ○ An interest in biology
- ○ An investigative spirit
- ○ Compassion
- ○ Courage
- ○ A love of wild plants and animals
- ○ A desire to travel all over the world

AMERICAN BULLFROG
amphibian

Origin: North America
New habitat: All over the world—except in Africa
Characteristics: The American bullfrog carries a dangerous fungal infection that puts other amphibians at risk.

EGYPTIAN GOOSE
bird

Origin: Egypt and parts of Africa south of the Sahara Desert
New habitat: Asia, Mauritius Islands, USA, Australia, and Europe
Characteristics: The Egyptian goose is an especially aggressive bird that may compete with native species for resources.

AMERICAN POND SLIDER
reptile

Origin: Some parts of the USA and Mexico
New habitat: All over the world!
Characteristics: The American pond slider is a large turtle that competes with native species for food as well as breeding and **basking sites.**

GRAY SQUIRREL
mammal

Origin: North America
New habitat: Europe and South Africa
Characteristics: Because it lacks predators outside North America, the gray squirrel can threaten the existence of native squirrels, such as the red squirrel of Europe.

GLOSSARY

Abyss -
Noun
A seemingly never-ending space or depth.

Albatross -
Noun
A large seabird with webbed feet and long, slender wings.

Algae -
Plural noun
A group of simple, typically aquatic plants, like seaweed.

Altitude -
Noun
The elevation of a place or object above the horizon.

Amphibian -
Noun
An animal such as a frog that can live on both land and in water.

Arid -
Adjective
Extremely dry due to little rainfall.

Artificially -
Adverb
Produced by humans, often mimicking something natural.

Atmosphere -
Noun
The gases that surround a planet.

Basking Sites -
Plural noun
Places where cold-blooded animals lie in the sun to regulate their body temperature.

Biofuels -
Plural noun
Fuels made from renewable sources, like plants.

Bioluminescence -
Noun
A glow produced by a chemical reaction within a living creature. Example: fireflies.

Carnival -
Noun
A festive season occurring in February and March marked by parades, dancing, and public street parties. (Called Carnaval in Brazilian Portuguese.)

Cells -
Plural noun
Tiny structural and functional units in every organism.

Climate -
Noun
The average weather of a region.

Cryogenic -
Adjective
Relating to the deep-freezing of bodies or objects for purposes of preservation.

Culling -
Verb
Selectively killing a wild animal species.

Cultivation -
Noun
The preparation of land for crop growth.

Deforestation -
Noun
The clearing and removal of forests from land.

Ecosystem -
Noun
A community of living organisms and nonliving components and the physical environment in which they all interact.

Electron Microscope -
Noun
A microscope that uses electron beams to magnify the structures of cells and other tiny specimens.

Extinct -
Adjective
Describing a species of plant, animal, insect, or any other living creature that no longer exists. Examples: the T-rex, saber-toothed tiger, and woolly mammoth.

Fossils -
Plural noun
The remains of an extinct animal, insect, or dinosaur preserved in a rock or other material.

Greenhouse Gas Emissions -
Plural noun
Gases like carbon dioxide, methane, and water vapor that are released into and absorbed by Earth's atmosphere.

Invertebrates -
Plural noun
Animals or insects that do not have a backbone. Examples: spiders, worms, and crabs.

Liquid Nitrogen -
Noun
Nitrogen at a very low temperature that is often used in the preparation of frozen desserts.

Mammals -
Plural noun
Warm-blooded animals that have fur or hair, give birth to live offspring, and produce milk to feed their young.

Meteorite -
Noun
A space rock that survives its entry into Earth's atmosphere such that part of it strikes the ground.

Millennia -
Plural noun
Thousands of years.

Organism -
Noun
A human, animal, plant, or single-celled life form.

Peninsula -
Noun
A piece of land almost entirely surrounded by water.

Phenomenon -
Noun
A rare fact, event, or situation that has been observed to happen.

Photosynthesis -
Noun
The process by which green plants convert sunlight into food.

Pollinators -
Plural noun
Animals or insects that help plants and flowers produce fruit and seeds. Example: honeybees.

Pollutants -
Plural noun
Substances that pollute something, such as the air or water.

Reptiles -
Plural noun
Scaly vertebrates that lay soft-shelled eggs. Examples: turtles, lizards, and snakes.

Samba -
Noun
A traditional Brazilian ballroom dance.

Sediments -
Plural noun
Solid materials that settle at the bottom of liquids.

Sirius -
Noun
A star of the Canis Major constellation that is larger, hotter, and brighter than the sun but much farther from Earth.

Spermatophytes -
Plural noun
Plants that produce seeds.

Stratosphere -
Noun
The second-lowest layer of Earth's atmosphere. At cruising altitude, most airplanes fly in the lower stratosphere.

Tectonic Plates -
Plural noun
Massive pieces of Earth's crust.

Textile -
Adjective
Relating to fabric or cloth.

Tracheophytes -
Plural noun
Plants, such as ferns, that contain vein-like cells for conducting water and minerals.

Trenches -
Plural noun
Long, narrow, deep ditches or gaps in the ocean floor.

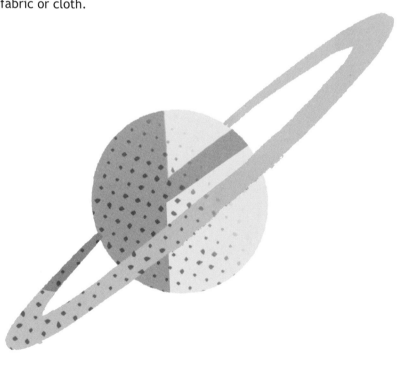

NOTES

Page 10:
Sea Level Rise.org. "There Are Four Main Causes of Sea Level Rise: Two Causes Are Global, And Two Are Local." Accessed September 2022. https://sealevelrise.org/causes/.

Yi, Shuang; Sun, Wenke; Heki, Kosuke; Qian, An. "An increase in the rate of global mean sea level rise since 2010." May 28, 2015.

Page 15:
NASA. "Gas Giant: A giant planet composed mainly of gas." March 22, 2021. https://exoplanets.nasa.gov/what-is-an-exoplanet/planet-types/gas-giant/.

NASA. "Neptune-like: Gaseous world around the size of Neptune." March 22, 2021. https://exoplanets.nasa.gov/what-is-an-exoplanet/planet-types/neptune-like/.

Page 22:
Ocean Conservancy. "The Problem with Plastics." Accessed September 2022. https://oceanconservancy.org/trash-free-seas/plastics-in-the-ocean.

United States Environmental Protection Agency. "National Overview: Facts and Figures on Materials, Wastes and Recycling." Accessed September 2022. https://www.epa.gov/facts-and-figures-about-materials-waste-and-recycling/national-overview-facts-and-figures-materials.

Page 39:
Slater, Thomas.; Lawrence, Isobel R.; Otosaka, Inès N.; Shepherd, Andrew; Gourmelen, Noel; Jakob, Livia; Tepes, Paul; Gilbert, Lin; Nienow, Peter. "Earth's ice imbalance." January 25, 2021. https://tc.copernicus.org/articles/15/233/2021/.

Page 58:
Animal Welfare Institute. "List of Endangered Species." Accessed September 2022. https://awionline.org/content/list-endangered-species.

Earth.org. "Sixth Mass Extinction of Wildlife Accelerating – Study." August 10, 2021. https://earth.org/sixth-mass-extinction-of-wildlife-accelerating/.

International Union for Conservation of Nature Red List. "The ICUN Red List of Threatened Species." Accessed September 2022. https://www.iucnredlist.org/.

Sofia E. Rossi

Sofia is a science communicator for the San Raffaele Hospital in Milan, Italy. She holds a degree in philosophy with a minor in neuroscience, and she is a tireless traveler. She loves to tell stories related to health, the environment, and the animal world.

Carlo Canepa

Carlo is a fact-checker for Pagella Politica, an Italian website dedicated to fact-checking politicians and stopping the spread of fake news. He holds a degree in philosophy, has written a book about soccer, and loves playing the guitar.

Luca Poli

Luca's work includes graphics, illustration, and everything in between. He loves comic books and music. No style is off-limits to him. Drawing is a bit like acting, and each project is its own unique drama.

Jobs of the Future copyright © 2022 by White Star s.r.l. All rights reserved. Printed in China. No part of this book may be used or reproduced in any manner whatsoever without written permission except in the case of reprints in the context of reviews.

Andrews McMeel Publishing
a division of Andrews McMeel Universal
1130 Walnut Street, Kansas City, Missouri 64106

www.andrewsmcmeel.com

i Lavori del Futuro was originally published in Italy in 2020 by White Star Kids®, a registered trademark property of White Star s.r.l.

Piazzale Luigi Cadorna, 6
20123 Milan, Italy
www.whitestar.it

22 23 24 25 26 SDB 10 9 8 7 6 5 4 3 2 1

ISBN: 978-1-5248-7095-9

Library of Congress Control Number: 2021946493

Made by:
King Yip (Dongguan) Printing & Packaging Factory Ltd.
Address and location of manufacturer:
Daning Administrative District, Humen Town
Dongguan Guangdong, China 523930
1st Printing – 12/20/21

ATTENTION: SCHOOLS AND BUSINESSES
Andrews McMeel books are available at quantity discounts with bulk purchase for educational, business, or sales promotional use. For information, please e-mail the Andrews McMeel Publishing Special Sales Department:
specialsales@amuniversal.com